# Where Time Hangs

MARK NUTTALL

CP
THE CHOIR PRESS

First published in the United Kingdom in 2024 by
The Choir Press

ISBN 978-1-78963-511-9

All images by Mark Nuttall

To my parents

# Contents

# Preface

The inspiration for writing these poems has arisen from reflections on the landscapes, histories, and contemporary circumstances of the northern Welsh-English borderlands and other parts of North Wales and Cheshire – with the occasional move across to Pennine slopes (places that may furnish ideas for more writing, who knows). They explore the wide and narrow spaces and cracks between presence and absence, history and modernity, nature and human intervention, capturing moments when time seems on occasion to stand still and, in a sense, to hang, as well as those more fleeting moments that just as easily slip away as soon as they appear.

The poems gathered together to form this collection began to take shape during more recent visits to the places that, I suppose in some ways, I will always think of as home. Even if that appears to be something strange to say, given my years rooted in other places. On those visits I had to attend to things that have, as they must also do for most of us at some point, preoccupied me. I found time – had to make time – to get away from those things. I had to make time for thinking, often on long walks in my old stomping grounds along coastline, canal tow paths, though woodland, in the hills and mountains. And there were shorter strolls I had to make, to reacquaint myself with all I had forgotten, around those churchyards where generations of us have been buried, across local fields, around the streets where my extended family lived, or down along the road to that incredible library and wonderful archive in the village.

No matter how long I would walk, the important thing was just to do so. Walking allowed my thoughts to form and settle. On intersections and thresholds, liminality, and questions of identity along and around the border that can be difficult to define. I reflected, in ways I have always tended to do – but have seldom, for whatever reason, allowed myself to do in recent years – on where my own past meets the present and the personal merges with the universal. And so, these poems deal with time, loss, memory, and landscape. They dwell on ancestry, family history, ghosts of the industrial past, connections to place, and all that is unspoken. In many ways, they are concerned with the relationships, ties, the fragments and brittle things that bind us to our surroundings and to each other.

I moved away from these places so long ago. But I return often. More so in the last few years. Much has changed. As if that is a surprise or revelation. I walk along streets once familiar, where banks, post offices, grocers, and butchers used to be, and visit those sites where industry was once dominant. More than that, many of the people I knew who lived and worked in those places have mostly gone too.

This has been a new form of writing for me. I allowed myself to draw on personal and collective memories and think about the ancestral legacies that, for better or worse, continue to have some bearing on daily life. And so these verses trace movement and flows in estuarine spaces of marsh, sand and mud, across the shifting and indeterminate ground between water and land. They cross upland areas covered with mine shafts and go deep in the underlands of lead mining and slate quarrying landscapes. They fix on the lines of history, memory, and identity, exploring how they linger in our lives and landscapes, including the underground extractive spaces that have shaped place and community, and the social and environmental effects that mining and quarrying have left us with. They are reflections on the transitional, the in-between places we move through – the ambiguous states, the moments of uncertainty and possibility we experience in the liminal spaces we cross over and move around in, and that often transform us. How is it, I have asked myself, that sometimes the most interesting things have been under your feet all the time?

My thanks go to David Onyett at The Choir Press for his thoughts and guidance as this collection moved through the publication process. And, as ever, I am thankful for the love, support and encouragement of Millie and Rohan, whose presence and understanding have been a constant source of strength and inspiration.

# Fleeting

# Yellow Weather Warning

I am haunted by persistent ghosts,
cranky, chunnering spirits in the walls,
that will not leave me alone.

With typical hubris and visceral delight
they pretend not to be there,
oozing through the door gaps,

lingering in the corners, dribbling,
slobbering down the stairs,
dragging themselves across the attic,

wrapping themselves, slithering, around
the brittle creaking bones of the house,
cracking, crunching, popping the joints,

sucking the velvety marrow, the silken stream,
enjoying the metallic warmth on their tongues,
raw, unrefined, filling the empty spaces.

Undeterred by the storm, swaggering,
ignoring the yellow weather warning,
they think I don't see them and can't hear

their jibber-jabber as they cling to the ceiling,
while the loose gutter bangs, bangs away,
furiously on the window frame.

Then in a brief lull, my heartbeat slows,
as the chatter dies down for a while.
I pick out your shuffle, that characteristic

trudge I thought had gone to ashes,
along the corridor in the small hours,
and hear the pull cord clicking

ratcheting, pipes knocking,
while the wind screams,
the rain hammers, and the trees snap.

# Limestone Escarpment

The afternoon sun drapes long shadows
over the limestone escarpment
we look out to from your window.
Although you cannot see it at all.

Or can you? I wonder what it is you can and do see,
what you feel, sense, imagine, think about.
What memories, if any, flutter, scratch,
panic, scream, desperately seeking light.

I tell you about the ancient textured stone.
This matters, even though you may not hear me,
nor understand, and have not known who I am
through all these long years that have passed.

If there is some consolation, my misplaced notion,
it is that you do not know he has gone.
But are you holding on for him
to walk through the door, as he did each day?

Perhaps he does come to you, and that is why
you are still here. He could be sitting at your side,
glancing across at me, trying to catch my eye
so that he can ask me to say you should let go.

I wonder what right we feel we have
to deny you this as you wither,
when you would choose to leave, released
from the shrunken frailty trapping your spirit.

Looking away, with characteristic cowardice,
from the other side of the bed to avoid his stare,
I read to you instead. Dipping into the stories,
those accounts of the things that really happened.

The lady in the lake; the giant carrying rocks
striding towards the strait, like a narrow brook, to Môn;
the dragons engaged in their perennial battle in the dark pool.
The silent ones, with their slippers made from beetle wings.

Later, I walk up to the craggy edge, to sit down there,
run my palms over the cool grit, skitter along the scree,
wander near the burial mound and contemplate
the singular, lonely path to the World's End.

I look back down to your window
from the weathered ridge where time hangs.
Wild thyme and leadwort cling defiantly in crevices.
Such perseverance. Such stubbornness.

# Passing Through The Lychgate

The clay pits and old landfill
were turned into a country park
a few years ago.

They now form part of a nature reserve
with wildflower meadows, woodland, trails.
Everything looks impressive.

Elided from the view,
there's no trace of the ruination,
churned earth, smokestacks, bent backs.

Unless you know where to look,
follow the memory lines, scratch your arms
and trip over the foundation stones.

I walk along the lane from the cottage
where my great grandmother once lived
down by the chapel.

A light rain shower has passed over,
the scent in the air is earthy, woody, loamy,
each step more squelchy

as the path turns to a claggy track
that takes me past the Mount Pool.
All puddles, sticky clay,

broken branches underfoot,
prickly bramble overhang,
fine hairs glistening on nettle tips,

through a passageway separating
houses from the smallholding
to the church on the common's edge.

The estuary to the northeast
is a shimmering ribbon
on this late February afternoon,

the higher hills in the west
a line of purple grey
like sombre low cloud.

On the edge of two worlds
in between,
yet part of the same.

Seeking solace
draws me here.
I'm sure it does.

Not faith, devotion,
nor the need for prayer.
Restoration perhaps.

Just passing through the lychgate,
then the roughly hewn feel
of the heavy oak door,

the creaking hinges,
the mustiness that greets me
as I enter the porch,

the chill rising
from the stone floor,
are almost enough to get me there.

# The Rusty Edges

There's one task that needs doing,
a circumstance I can no longer put off.
I draw breath and go to the garage one evening
to clatter my way through the aftermath.

Tools are scattered on benches,
some stored neatly in boxes,
each a memory of his quiet projects,
with their tales of woodwork, hammer and nail.

Rusty blade edges, worn handles
I struggle to identify as hickory or ash,
and I notice the tarnished metal,
the crusty soil on tines, blunt shears,

brushes in jars of mineral spirits,
stem injectors, weed wipers,
prickle strips, pumice powder
and polishing wheels.

All are blemished relics, a reminder of the corrosion.
I know that if I am to cherish these artefacts
of his soft presence, his pottering,
then we have to cast away the iron.

We must let go and give them away.
It still feels like a betrayal,
severing this connection,
slicing through the muscle

with its bony attachment,
allowing the essence to leak
through the cracks and dissipate.
Yet I sort and gather.

# Coastal Drift

Each time I dwell on your passing
my thoughts split into slivers
that embed themselves in places
I thought I could not feel pain.

So I go along the coastline,
to contemplate the lateral movement
of sand, silt, and pebbles,
ocean currents, waves, and tides.

Prevailing wind patterns,
dynamics altered by breakwaters,
groynes, seawalls,
erosion, sedimentation.

It seems such a pointless effort,
this grasping for the numinous,
falling into something vast and endless,
searching for a glimmer of the infinite.

This only prolongs an elusive endeavour.
A longing beyond all comprehension,
caught in the hairline fracture
between presence and absence.

# Masarn

Gloomy shapes crawl out
gather, chafe and flit
around the streetlights
as the evening settles in.

There's a distant mumble
that fades quickly.
Something restless stirs
unseen, unknown.

It makes it harder to evade
those buried emotions
I'd rather not bring to the surface
as I approach the house.

I turn the key in the lock
step into the hallway
and shiver, taking in
that familiar fustiness.

I stand in the stillness,
in that dimness,
for a moment,
or longer, it seems,

then reach for the switch,
turn on the lights,
and check each room
one final time.

The silence, the emptiness
are scarred by absence,
while the air hangs, thick
with stale memories

and those heavy
unspoken words
that sear into the gashes
of this quiet ache.

# Pilgrim Trail

The solitude of the trail prepared me
for this moment of stillness,
stepping into a timeless
sanctuary, inviting pause.

Standing by the edge,
the stream bubbling up,
reflecting the candle flicker,
I grasped its significance for the first time.

Belief, reverence,
the water washing over souls,
cleansing sorrows,
renewing spirits.

In that moment, understanding
why pilgrims come here,
seekers of hope,
finding peace in sacred space.

# The Flooded Land

Storms take.

Yet they also reveal
the lost and submerged.

Like the great forest
petrified beneath the sea.

Although, it should be said,
the land was never forgotten
by the old stories,

those telling of home, hearth,
flourishing fields,
fecundity and mead.

And the sound of the bells
ringing underwater.

# Rabbit Skins

Old rags, old bones
any old iron
rabbit skins
anything broken.

I would look out for the cart
pulled by the doe eyed horse
to come along our street.
Their arrival my own adventure.

Cracked crocks, rusting pots
any old clothes
raven wings
everything taken.

Wheels creaking, feathers flying
from the gunny sacks,
scrap rattling, coal scattering,
grease clinging stubbornly.

Rabbit skins
any lost things
magpie nests
wishes unspoken.

I would follow along for a while,
wide-eyed, and dream of the world
beyond rooftop and lane,
out there, wild and open.

Rabbit skins
old tin cans
rags and bones
anything forsaken.

# Washed Away

Reaching the smugglers' cave
I take the higher ground
and leave the foreshore
as the incoming tide
begins to claim the beach.

I glance back along to where
the footprints I made
are now washed away by foam,
every trace erased
as if I had never been there at all.

# Surface Moulter

I wake gasping for breath.
Rasping, grabbing for it,
as the heavy sense of dread
over everything being all so fleeting
presses down on my chest.

I reach out for my exoskeleton
lying where I left it on the moist sand
when I crawled out of my own body,
but I can no longer fit inside,
and the new shell has yet to form.

Being here on the surface is a risk,
and I cannot bury myself deep enough.
If I could choose the skin I need to grow,
it would be something I would not have
to shed every now and then.

# Unravelling

We are witness
to the world unravelling,
uneasy and suffering
from the discomfort
of the realisation that nature
no longer guides
our days with precision.
If it ever did.

Once, we looked to the sky
for familiar signs,
for reassurance in the chaotic.
Now the weather shakes us
with the erratic patterns we ignored,
the things we took for granted.
The clouds twist and churn,
confounding our expectations.

The Romantic poets,
with their odes
to nature's wonder,
the painters
with their mountain
studies and sketches
of dove's plume
and pewter gleam

sought the luminescent
and sublime
in storms and sunsets,
in untouched landscapes,
finding manifestations
of the divine
in every rustling leaf
and babbling brook.

Wordsworth, revisiting
the banks of the Wye,
wrote in 'Tintern Abbey'
of tranquil restoration,
of a profound connection
between humanity
and the natural world.

But, then again,
it was an imaginary scene,
a cultivation of the picturesque
ignoring the charcoal smoke
and vagrant dwellers.

Could a Wordsworth ever,
even dare, compose such lines again,
knowing the landscapes
that inspired such introspection
are marred in the Anthropocene
by the scars of our presence?
The sublime, it seems,
has given way to the apocalyptic.

Has it been anything other?
The deep mysteries
must surely still be there,
submerged under the layers
of our own making.

# Layers

# Fireclay

Do you remember the thick smoke,
the chimneys, those sooty works
with their moulds and kilns
where housing estates now spread?

Clay made this town,
defined it, breathed life into it,
brought families into the world
from below ground.

Encroachment around the mountain
happened first for the potteries,
the landless attracted to the outcrops,
mauling over the near-surface deposits

digging through material
washed in by glacial drift,
living with the mudstone,
making course earthenware,

jugs, pans, great butter pots,
dishes, ridge tiles, flowerpots,
tobacco pipes, sugar bowls, salt bowls.
Then came the bricks and tiles.

Great open excavations at every turn
dug into the shale clays
to get to the purer stuff
for making the common brick.

Blue and yellow from the marl layers
to make the pale red colour,
then, going lower down,
toiling in the grit and grime,

to the dark clay, thick and malleable,
for the firebrick, tempered
in the searing heat, turning paler,
from the dark carbonaceous matter.

Coal hauled up from beneath the sea
brought down from the north point,
extracted from the local measures,
making the burnt woods, the spoil tips.

Everything transported to the coast
on rickety rails.
Gears, steam,
metal and motion.

People in the churches and chapels
on rickety legs.
Hymns croaking,
prayers hoping.

# The Deeper Levels

With each step below ground
I have this indescribable feeling
of going further than before
into something immense
where everything is hazy and blurred.

I'm frequently wet before I get
even halfway down the shaft
into this mere piercing of the crust
and this way shortens life
that much I know too well.

The world above, indifferent,
will breathe, move without me,
but I was down here that time
when we heard the dripping
before that sudden rush.

The water burst along the level,
then once it subsided and drained away
we scraped at the hole, crawled through,
walked along the river bed
and looked around in wonder.

# Llechi

In the shadow of the slate
life was tethered to home
hillside and deep time

hard to think about it now
but the stories persist,
essential to keep it all alive

rhythmic thud, pickaxe echo
in the ancient silence
dim tallow light flickering

digging, extracting
splitting, spitting,
coughing up the dust

carving, coaxing
layers relinquishing
with each muscle strain

hauling, dressing
transforming rough stone
from mountain to path and roof

slate made things weathertight
yet silicosis would still get them
if a momentary slip didn't.

# Night Rustle

Oh, yes, you've told me that story
and I'll hear it again
because it never wears thin
when you tell it your way

and I need to be reminded
of how the living was tough
in that moldering farmstead
on the bare hill along by the falls

the endless struggle
with scant reprieve
from the rough
and from the ready

earth floor
mud wattled roof
smoke wafting
through the partitions.

They'd be up there grazing
on the adjoining slopes
and he would go about stealthily
seeking out the ewes and the wethers

just one from here
one from there,
one more from here,
just one more from there.

Oh, no, they wouldn't be missed
spirited away in the night
by desperate hands
that would spin hope from the fleece

make a life of sorts from the mutton
happily taken through the back door
and they paid a decent price
then, whispers in the chapel, inn chatter

ease off now, lie low for a while
some toil and moil in the quarry
because there was no money
coming from that scraggy patch

then up again
back in the damp
to take and shake
someone else's livelihood

just one from here
one from there,
one more from here,
just one more from there

until they started to talk
about the missing
still present
through their absence.

Ah, yes, what a mistake
to think no-one would notice
their disappearance, but how foolish
to imagine they didn't feel their *cynefin*.

They were not in the habit
of straying far from their own ground,
so that waiting for a train one morning
down on the branch line

with some silver and gold in his pocket
and a memorandum book
it was the two sheep with him
their out of place look

that alerted the *heddwas*
others were found in the butcher's field
the rest here and there
in various spots along the coast

one from here over there
one from there over here,
a few more here,
a few more from there.

They were ear-marked,
but they knew them alright,
by sight, knew their faces,
recognised them by their countenance.

Everyone regarded him as virtuous,
thought of him as honest, sober,
and with his brother the minister
standing up there on Sundays,

but the judge disagreed;
no doubt born of good character,
he became lost on his descent
into cruel dishonesty.

Oh, yes, he said
the jury had arrived
at a sensible conclusion,
and it was his imperative duty

not merely to punish a crime
with five years of penal servitude
but to send a warning to others
stifled under a heather thatch.

# Inscription

Walking around the churchyard
I go in search of a headstone,

a lineage, bloodline, hoping to engage in
a silent conversation with the past.

Nearby, two women stand
by the memorial wall,

their heads lowered
having just placed fresh flowers.

The quiet moments are punctuated
by joy and sorrow,

resignation and defeat,
love and loss.

Memories linger
as time fades and blurs,

turning those ancestral echoes
into a soft hum.

I find the grave,
it's nothing remarkable,

I can just about make out the words,
and trace them with my finger,

while wondering
about the bones below.

The worn inscription
is mottled with moss,

much like the emerging pattern
on the back of my hand.

Time is etched on skin
and on sandstone.

It speaks of an end, a brevity
that is somewhat relieving.

There is a strange comfort in this feeling
of everything slipping away,

a harsh reminder, if ever one is needed,
of our momentary existence.

# By The Murky Channel

Beneath the smog-stained sky
by the murky channel,
hardly a river at this point.

Across the bridge and along
from where they made the galvanized steel
in the furnaces on the reclaimed marshland.

I imagine him working there
on that morning in February 1915
with yellowing fingers,

in that creosote coated shed,
carefully tended and smoke-filled,
cutting and trimming the hide.

Moulding it to fit the foot,
hammering tacks along the heel,
punching the eyelet holes.

Stitching the sole,
stretching the tongue
and all the time thinking

of that walk he was going to take
later that day to where they had set up,
there in the local hall,

so that he could do what he felt,
he thought, was his duty
and answer the call.

# December Morning

I walk along the road
from my parents' house
through the cutting
to the bus stop

squeezed in there
on the narrow pavement,
scratched sign hidden
by the cedar hedge.

The breeze is salt scented
retaining the lingering
presence of autumn
and I breathe it in.

The periwinkle sky
is streaked with jasmine
and sun glow, so perhaps
winter is not too far away.

The bus comes into view
rounds the bend
ambles down the hill
its destination sign alternating,

between Caer in Welsh
Chester in English,
as if going to two places
but one and the same.

It feels good sitting here
rambling down the long lane
going down the wood lane
looking across to the wide plain.

Quiet chatter, accents affirming
this border place is somewhere
neither here nor there, yet all around
life is interwoven, threading through.

At journey's end I saunter
for a while and then head
to the Christmas market
at the town hall square.

I make my way through the crowd,
wander around the stalls
watching the vendors selling
festive decorations, Welsh knitwear

artisan crafted cheese
from Gwynedd
from Cheshire
speciality coffees

nutty English ales
crusty pies
fiery, fruity jams
hog roasts.

I linger at the Cathedral stall
and buy two small angels
hand carved in Bethlehem
from olive wood.

Later, on the bus back up to the high pasture
I take the angels from their brown paper bag
to admire, wonder at.
They are polished and smooth.

# Rubble

Beneath all that rubble
a quiet rage festers, smouldering
under the accumulated debris
of the things we inherit.

We keep piling it on,
plugging the gaps with stones
and lumps of concrete,
blocking the air,

smothering, suffocating
any chance of release,
pushing those burdens deeper,
ignoring the suppuration,

burying the memories
of those who keep scratching
their fingertips to the bone
to reach the surface.

It is time, I think,
to claw back the rubble,
reach down, grab their wrists
and help them climb out.

# Lingering Lines

This is where uncommon lives find sanctuary,
in the pioneering green and salt.

Slender hare's ear, flat-sedge,
Piddock beds in ancient clay,

cordgrass, glasswort, seablite,
Sea purslane unfolding,

Portland spurge, dune fescue,
white horehound,

Seaside centaury, ephemeral fragile beauty,
petalwort unfurling in the slack.

Grayling butterfly feasting on Sea-holly,
sand lizard rustle, listen for the natterjack.

But other things gather here,
circulate and persist.

Lead permeates, settles in the soil.
Particulates float, swirl in the air.

Radionuclides seep
through the salt marsh,

into the halophytes,
then go flying off with the little egret.

Pesticides cling to the sediment
sinking, spreading in granular beds

burrowing down
with the Razor clams,

their fragile shells washing up on shore,
breaking down into sand.

Dust infiltrates our lungs,
trace metals in our blood

tracing them
to industrial dreams,

the copper, the steel,
the measures, the seams.

Everything lingers in the earth,
in our bodies, in the phlegmatic,

lurking, leeching,
following down

the patrilineal paths,
across the matrilineal maps

into the present.
And on we go,

intoxicated by the toxic cocktail,
hacking up our inheritance.

# Crossings

porous movement,
water seeping through,
crossings.

border people
back and forth,
interfluvial families.

we know who we are,
moving through places
where histories, stories,

identities, dialects co-mingle,
where words are mangled
when gobbling the lobsgows.

lives bound up
with the metalliferous
once shackled to lead mines,

brickworks, collieries,
smelters, shipyards,
marked by limestone,

fireclay, chalk, shale,
smoke, dust, copper, steel,
mud and the silty estuary.

sweat, suffocating heat,
hands split
and bleeding

the silence came,
sudden and swift
the air reeking still

of loss,
grind
and grief.

earth reshaping,
nature reclaiming
there's a new wild

emerging amidst
the ruination
of this storied landscape.

So, we went to the hall
to hear about the project
intending to capture

and store carbon dioxide
mitigating climate change
through systemic transitions

replacing fossil fuel
dependent systems
envisioning

a carbon-neutral world
advancing towards sustainability
sequestering $CO_2$

in subsurface formations
a pipeline running below
our homes, our schools, our fields

depleted gas reservoirs
beneath the seabed
as secure repositories

geological integrity
ensuring containment
Earth's stratigraphy

offering hope as
a burial ground for a future
less burdened by emissions.

# Stacksteads

Small farms, spinners, dyers,
weavers bent over looms,
crafting with land, wool,
flax and fustian on Pennine slopes.

Children born, some dying, some growing,
agrarian to industrial transformation,
gentle whirring to power loom roaring,
mass production factories rising.

Machine-breaking riots,
fear gripped the air,
life was on the cusp of change
with looms shattering, mills burning.

Stacksteads felt the fire.
Dragoons, artillery, six dead, the ire,
thirty-five men, seven women
sentenced to death, others to prison.

Living through upheaval,
the family was not untouched,
by the flames of change.
But then he came along.

The mist veils were lifted
from the higher ridges,
his eyes traced rugged outlines,
sheep dotted on green below.

Paint blended the sky in gold
and deep blue. The landscape unfolded
in hues as the river's gentle flow
stretched across the canvas.

# Stone Flakes

Flakes and roughouts
lie scattered in the field,
reached by the old track

through the gorse
along past the derelict
family homestead.

Remnants of tools
and weapons carved
from the bones of the mountain.

Hands, rough and skilled,
chiselled material
in the axe factory

chipping from the scree and crags
discarding imperfect shards,
coaxing the raw stone

from the sacred places
into works of wonder,
shaping their world.

Learning to read the rock,
the craft was nurtured
in quarries and mines.

Five thousand years
of journey lines across the land,
in the sand, deep below.

Ancient paths and trails
linking valleys, coast,
hills and home.

# Indeterminate

# Estuary

The ground is soft, spongy, brackish,
salt marsh and water interlace,
vanishing from my line of sight
with the mist shroud descending.

Mud grips, my boots stick,
earthy root fingers curl tight and grasp
as I make my way to a firmer path
just when the drizzle begins to seep in.

The wind picks up, then straightens its back,
there's a sharp edge to the crack
while I press on over to the low sea wall
near the high tide roost on the reed beds.

The waterscape here is ever shifting,
I can feel a storm surge coming
and I'm suddenly aware of how absence
can be such a reliable companion.

I pass the wooden stumps that hint of a past
of busy wharves, coastal trade, hopes made,
when vessels, some built on these banks,
squeezed though channels of sand and silt.

Lead smelting works, copper mills,
villages buzzed with industry, with products
shipped from the Greenfield Dock
to Liverpool, then reaching far-off shores.

Guinea rods, manillas, trinkets,
brass neptune for the African trade,
currency for human souls,
pots and pans to cook the stockfish

split and dried on the racks along the edges
of the cold fjords. The cruel, dark history
is embedded in the mudflats
dissonant with invertebrate stridulation.

Worms, bivalves, amphipods feed the fish,
the waterbirds, the sky.
Beneath the tides the nursery lies
for lamprey, salmon, shad and eels.

Sailing from The Holy, fishers and cocklers,
move around crossing the liminal spaces
marked by water, mud, and dune,
navigating shallows slowed by sediment,

while out there in the dark brine,
low level cloud deceiving like a sly whisper,
the slow wing barge is making its way
north through the gut.

# Surge/Retreat

Water meets land. As the rain
soaks the gravel it bleeds, runs off
at the margins, into the ditches,

when at first the way appeared
to stretch before me as a passage
that would lead through upheaval,

a route across this terrain of loss
towards some sense of acceptance
acknowledging that grief has its own tides,

the lows, the highs, powerful and enduring,
of understanding how this unsettling feeling
has its own rhythm of surge and retreat.

And so, I try to breathe, then exhale
and release some of the weight
       I carry.

# The Toothed Skerry

I wonder about the origin
of these place names.
Norse, Old English, Welsh,
some with an etymology
no longer known.

Hylde, high ground;
holr, hollow; Linga, heath;
Meols, sand dunes;
Mockbeggar.
What dereliction.

The village of commotion,
places of fuss, bustle,
trouble, agitation;
the furnace on the banks,
the green field, the deep, the swash.

I wonder about us living here
down the generations,
working the mills, down at the forge,
the grime and grit, heat seeping
through the pores, the air thick and raw.

I wonder about those who came here,
travelling on these marshes,
sailing through the channels,
getting wrecked on the mudbanks,
floundering in the hyper-tidal.

I wonder about the treachery
of these waters, the deception
of the shifting sands
the ambush and the crossing
of the constable sondes.

And down near the water's edge,
under a simmering sky, just along
from the roosting in the saltings,
tender fingers of mist are pricked
by the sharpness of the toothed skerry.

# Triturus cristatus

Out of the pond,
up and along,
glistening, you glide.

Hunting, seeking,
foraging by night
going underground

in mammal burrows,
slipping between cracks by day
finding refuge beneath rocks,

under logs and debris,
crawling out
from the leaf litter.

Your orange belly, the black spots,
a fierce warning
proclaiming your toxicity.

Insinuating your warty,
slippery self into the labyrinthine,
defying the twists and turns

of local bureaucracy,
frustrating the ambitions
of architects, builders, road makers.

Charismatic amphibian,
challenging blooms
of concrete and asphalt.

# Forming

Darkness trickles into light
as I move through
a half-dreamed world
squinting to bring it all
into sharper focus
while everything shifts.

I feel adrift
stumbling along
with the tilt of the path
towards the unseen
the unfixed, the fluid,
the indeterminate.

My surroundings float,
refusing to conform
to the map in my head,
but through the disarray
there are things out there
assuming new form.

# Early Coastal Light

Do you ever feel
you want to taste the ocean?

Let that briny tang,
the salt on your tongue,

take you to places
far flung, unimagined.

Beyond the scope
of your land bound vision,

across the shadowed waves,
into the misty grey nothing,

where the horizon drops without warning
over the precipice?

I feel this way, right now,
in this early coastal light.

Standing on the shoreline
while the water nudges my heels,

as I reach out, stretching
for the sun's first touch.

# Gazing Upon Ruins

The romantic traveller crossed the border
on foot, with quill, brush, and easel
in search of spectacular landscapes,
eager to sit among stone circles,
megaliths and ruined castles.

The crumbling monument, on its lofty rock,
decaying, overgrown with vegetation
was gazed upon as enchantment itself,
more than a curiosity suitable for canvas,
it was evidence of the antiquity.

Some came across the estuary
in two-masted boats
with a fine wind on a fair day
and proceeded to examine the battlements
before seeking country fare and well-aired beds.

The adventurous traveller went deeper
in search of wild and rugged scenes,
dark and silent lakes, the savage myths
the true, authentic, the real,
not just the picturesque.

They scribbled in diaries, wrote letters,
found inspiration for their watercolours,
made time for replenishment with *cwrw*,
enjoyed the essence of hospitality,
good manners and cultural immersion.

Cymraeg was considered a living artefact
embedded in the very landscape,
running through its arteries,
expressing its ancient history,
stitching it all together.

# The In-Between

I do not consider
the border as marked
by the line on the map
to be a sharp divide

a suggestion of identity
restricted and confined
within the pages
of a single narrative.

I see it offering something else.
Spaces carved in the heart
of the in-between,
inviting discovery.

Allowing me to see
who I am, all I can be,
and what my surroundings
are always becoming.

# Along The Grave's Ridge

It is said there
was a cromlech
near the farm
where the big stones
lie scattered.

One stands out
tall, broad, imposing,
but it's often hidden
by the Devil's cloak.

Other traces appear lost
and the map bemuses,
so the giant's grave
remains elusive
while the hauntings linger.

# Gathering

The tide pulls back slowly
revealing grooves and channels.
Wind smooth as sea glass,
sunlight on lustrous grains.

Mudflats glisten,
ridged shells exposed,
rolling downshore
along the water's edge.

Shore crabs scuttle and advance,
oystercatchers come to graze.
The pickers wade in,
baskets slung, nets ready.

# Beluga Dance

I look skyward to witness the
Beluga dance over Hope's crest,
with engine roar above the spinning world
and its entanglements of fate and chance.
In essence, life is quite the marvel.

# Soundings

The vessel slips
into the shale grey grip
of the awakening day

and out on the open water
to peer within the submerged
inverted, unseen world

of valleys and peaks
sculpted by grinding ice
untouched by sunlight

echo sounder, modern diviner
casting acoustic waves,
pulsing into the void

bringing surface and seabed
into dialogue, tracing lines,
contours, trenches,

ridges, plateaus, hidden depths
soundings, sketching,
reading the formations.

# Brittle

# Outcrops

I cherish this plateau
with its outcrops

the crop outs, the bare rock,
limestone, chert, the millstone grit.

Carboniferous backbone,
etched with the lesions of extraction.

Traces of shallow surface workings
reveal themselves in open cuts

along the lines of the ore veins,
each fissure and crack,

channels sculpted through rock,
in a search for hidden riches.

watercourses disrupted,
contaminated lifelines.

Wonderful for fossil hunting.

# Underneath

When I walk
across the mountain
I think of what
they imagined below.

It would have been
like embarking
on an expedition
across the unruly ocean

as they set out
to explore, investigate
order, explain, claim
subdue, possess,

with their maps, optics
and representations
for the digging down
through the underneath.

But it was different frontier,
no open space of air and light,
only darkness, walls of rock.
An immense subterranean world.

# Helygain

Be attentive to what is under foot
at all times when walking across
this landscape of striations
craters and folds.

It is easy to trip, stumble
into ankle-twisting depressions
if one departs from the paths
and sheep tracks.

    And under foot.

Tunnels wind
through a recessed
world of murmurs
and drips.

The chill seeps
from stone
and the air clings
with damp.

As miners dug,
carving passages,
searching for ore bodies,
vertical shafts pierced the earth,

horizontal levels branched out,
intersecting the bones of the land,
reaching mineral veins, cross-courses,
waters rising.

Ore bodies discovered,
worked until depletion,
burrowing, excavation,
tunnelling, unveiling

chambers, caves, caverns,
vertical pots, rift passages,
avens, watercourses, lakes,
a subsurface extractive zone.

Long Rake
Old Rake
Silver Rake
Deep Level

Pant-y-pydew
Pant-y-pwll-dwr
Chwarel Las
Powell's Lode

China Rake
Pant-y-ffrith
Caleb Bell.

They spoke
of others
nameless, felt,
remaining unseen.

Shadow companions
working alongside
in the silence
dissolving the line

between the breath
of the living
and the pulse
of the deep.

# Quercus

Ancient oak roots
anchoring life

twisting turning
grasping

reaching down through
the thirsty soil

remembering drought
remembering rain

Quiet earth
Warm earth

Dry ground
Root vein

# Iced Over Track

Shifting ice, crackle, groan,
cautious, sliding step.
Fleeting cloud, time paused,
hold my breath.

Heart steady, eyes scanning,
seeking solid ground.
Morning sun, distant glow,
subtle tease of warmth.

Cold air biting, frozen moment,
fragile stillness.
Heavy branches, crystal laden.
Life suspended.

# Sea Stack

Sea stack rising.
What a solitary, defiant
gnarled earth bone.

Waves retreat,
return, caress,
grind.

The wind etches,
writes, strips,
smoothes.

Decay, disintegration
drift, dissolution
washing in, washing away.

That's the extraordinary thing
about weathering.

It happens unnoticed
until its effects are apparent.

# Stickleback

Silver gleam,
flash of red and green.
The bony plated reed weaver
catches my eye.

No scales, skimming
from the nest tunnel.
The three-spined tadpole chaser
deftly evades the pond dipper.

Tiny bubbles rise,
ripples spread wide
across the surface shimmer.
Swift, elusive fish darting.

# The Works Under The Valley

They built the works on a foundation
of nineteenth-century lead dreams,
along by the meandering river.
Mustard gas and secrets stored in tunnels.

Names etched in the annals of atomic lore
tested theories in the quiet valley.
Uranium enrichment, gaseous diffusion,
isotope separation, pressurised against membranes.

Rhydymwyn
Manhattan
Los Alamos
Tube Alloys.

Science was hidden from view
in underground chambers, as the sheep grazed
and the world teetered above,
looking into the abyss at something terrifying.

# Fragments

Fragments, remains
of larger objects left behind
remnants, artefacts
more than residual scraps.

Intimations, glimpses
offered of past lives
exposed, excavated
unearthed.

Shards of glass, sherds of pottery
pieces of tooth, bone, fossils
evidence of animals,
bodies in the peat layers.

Fading strips of manuscript
shedding light on moments,
events, evidence of things
hoped for, discarded.

Memories of work,
traces of fences, walls,
stone columns, foundations,
materials buried, submerged.

Fragments left behind in the wake
of a cataclysmic weather event
or fire, or dug from the rubble
of homes, shattered, silent.

Isolated stands in stretches
of old growth stubble
cleared by chainsaws,
life severed at its roots.

Fragments can also be extractions
drawn with precision,
tissue samples, genes,
stem cells. Family histories.

Fragments are usually smaller,
more scattered than other remnants
visible in the form of ruins,
pieces much harder to unearth.

Or bring to the surface, requiring
some effort of reassembling
to get an idea of just exactly where
they would once fit in with the whole.

But on its own what does
a fragment say?

# Litterfall

Dappled light filters through
detritus gathers on the forest floor
lichen threads lace the bark
fungi sprout in hidden corners
moss blankets, spider silk
filaments weaving through the soil
breaking down, fragmenting
earthworm castings
nutrients bleeding deep
leaching, plant root succour
humification, building up
new life emerges from decay.

# Dredging

The steel-mouthed giant
is gorging on the bed,
tearing at the sediment flesh,
scooping tendons of sand and silt.

Incision, calculation,
slicing through.
Intrusion, preservation
access and exclusion.

Tides shift, the estuary breathes.
Then everything settles,
veiling the incursions,
obscuring the interventions

without removing the scars we leave.
And on we go dredging, lacerating,
filling the wounds with salt.
Tugging at the undercurrent.

# Old Boat

Weathered and worn, the old boat rests
on the edge of the marsh, its blue paint brittle,
curled and peeling like aged skin,
exposing the wrinkled and cracked belly timbers.

In the solitude of its abandonment
air, water, and earth are working steadily
to ensure its inevitable decomposition.
But there's no great hurry to soften the splintered edges.

In the meantime, the old boat comes in useful
as a place of rest for Black-tailed Godwit, Sedge Warblers,
the occasional Sparrowhawk, Twite feeding on seeds,
and a base for the fishing operations of Great Crested Grebe.

Weathered and worn, the old boat rests
on the East Atlantic Flyway, its blue paint peeling,
cradling life, easing death, witnessing rebirth.

www.ingramcontent.com/pod-product-compliance
Lightning Source LLC
LaVergne TN
LVHW010307070426
835511LV00027B/3497